DORLING KINDERSLEY ⏣ EYEWITNESS GUIDES

SHAKESPEARE

Boy
player

Hornbook

Quill pens

Horn
inkwells

Nine men's morris game

Hautboy,
or shawm

Model of the
Globe theatre

Hare

Schoolboy

Spanish galleon

Skull used as a prop

SHAKESPEARE

Written by
PETER CHRISP

Photographed by
STEVE TEAGUE

Swordfighting
in *Hamlet*

A Dorling Kindersley Book

Black rat

Crown used as a prop

Cockerel used in cock-fights

Travelling library

Sword and dagger

Bunch of garden herbs

Bottom from *A Midsummer Night's Dream*

Elizabethan noblewoman

DK

LONDON, NEW YORK, MUNICH, MELBOURNE, and DELHI

Project editor Louise Pritchard
Art editor Jill Plank
Editor Annabel Blackledge
Assistant art editors Kate Adams, Yolanda Carter
Senior editors Monica Byles
Senior art editors Jane Tetzlaff, Clare Shedden
Category publisher Jayne Parsons
Senior managing art editor Jacquie Gulliver
Senior production controller Kate Oliver
Picture researcher Franziska Marking
Picture librarians Sally Hamilton, Rachel Hilford
DTP designers Matthew Ibbotson, Justine Eaton
Jacket designer Dean Price

PAPERBACK EDITION
Managing editor Andrew Macintyre
Managing art editor Jane Thomas
Senior editor Kitty Blount
Senior art editor Martin Wilson
Editor Karen O'Brien
Designer Floyd Sayers
Picture research Bridget Tilly
DTP designer Siu Yin Ho

This Eyewitness ® Guide has been conceived by
Dorling Kindersley Limited and Editions Gallimard

Hardback edition first published in Great Britain in 2002.
This edition published in Great Britain in 2003 by
Dorling Kindersley Limited, 80 Strand, London WC2R 0RL

A CIP catalogue record
for this book is available
from the British Library.

ISBN-13: 978-1-4053-0093-3

Colour reproduction by
Colourscan, Singapore
Printed in Hong Kong
by Toppan

See our complete
catalogue at
www.dk.com

Contents

Lute

Shakespeare's birthplace

WILLIAM SHAKESPEARE was born in 1564, in the small town of Stratford-upon-Avon, England. At that time, Stratford had only eight or nine streets and fewer than 1,500 inhabitants. It was a market town, where the local farmers could bring their crops, animals, and other goods to sell. William's exact birth date is not known, but it would have been shortly before his christening, which took place on 26 April. He was born into a prosperous middle-class family. His father, John, was one of Stratford's leading men and served on the council that governed the town. He made his living as a glove-maker, and also dealt in wool and timber.

A BARD IS BORN
William was born in this house in Henley Street, Stratford. The house has now been turned into the Birthplace Museum. The rooms have been furnished to show how they would have looked in Shakespeare's time.

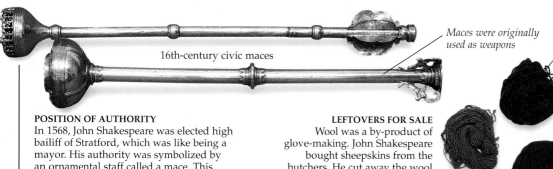

16th-century civic maces

Maces were originally used as weapons

Blue dye came from the woad plant

Yellow dye came from the weld plant, or "dyer's broom"

Red dye came from madder roots

POSITION OF AUTHORITY
In 1568, John Shakespeare was elected high bailiff of Stratford, which was like being a mayor. His authority was symbolized by an ornamental staff called a mace. This was carried before him in processions by an officer called a sergeant at mace.

LEFTOVERS FOR SALE
Wool was a by-product of glove-making. John Shakespeare bought sheepskins from the butchers. He cut away the wool and prepared the skins so that he could use them for his gloves. He then sold the wool to Stratford's dyers and weavers. It was dyed using a variety of local plants and woven into cloth.

16th-century velvet and satin mittens embroidered with flowers

GLOVE STORY
In the 16th century, wealthy people wore fashionable, beautifully embroidered gloves like these mittens. People also wore gloves for warmth and protection. John Shakespeare may have sold embroidered gloves, but would not have made them himself. Embroidery was done mainly in the home by women.

WORK FROM HOME
John Shakespeare's workshop was situated in the house in Henley Street. He prepared the animal skins, then cut and sewed them into gloves. John probably also sold his gloves, purses, and other leather goods from his workshop.

Walls were covered with decorative tapestries or cheaper painted cloth

Straw was used as a mattress

CROWDED HOUSE

William grew up in a crowded house, and probably shared a space-saving "truckle bed" like this with some of his brothers and sisters. In the daytime, the lower bed could be wheeled right under the upper one. In Shakespeare's day, it was normal for children to keep warm by sharing the same bed.

MOTHER'S ROOM

This is thought to be the room where John's wife Mary gave birth to William and his seven brothers and sisters. It has been furnished to show how it may have looked after the birth of William's brother Richard in 1574. A cradle stands by the bed, and the basket is full of strips of linen called swaddling bands used to wrap babies.

Knobs and grooves carved by hand on a lathe

BUILT TO IMPRESS

As a small child, William probably sat in a high chair just like this. The elaborate decoration would have made it an expensive item of furniture. The carving was not for the baby's benefit, but to impress neighbours and visitors. Parents who could afford such a fancy high chair would have given an impression of wealth and good taste.

FAMILY MISFORTUNES

For a time, John Shakespeare's businesses were very successful, and he could afford expensive tableware, like these pewter dishes in the hall of the Birthplace Museum. In 1576, however, John's businesses began to fail. He got into debt and lost his position of importance in the town. William, who was 12 years old at the time, must have been affected by his father's money problems. When he grew up, he would work to restore his family's fortunes.

Going to school

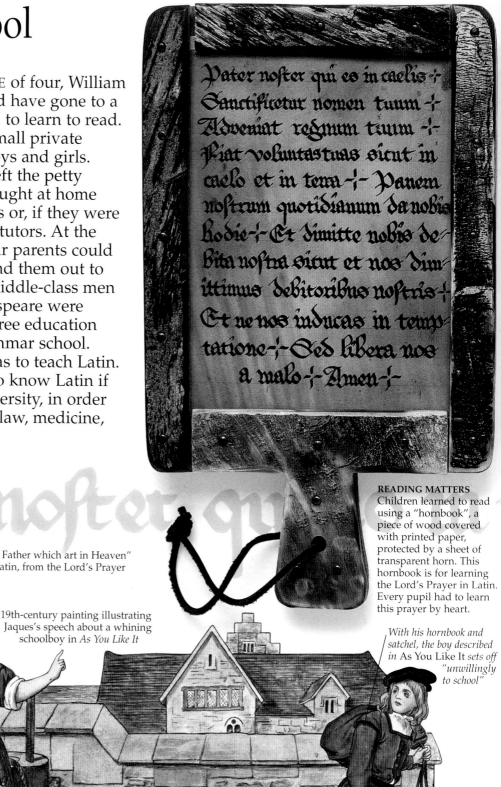

BIRCH BEATING
Schoolmasters always carried a bundle of birch twigs. This was used to beat pupils when they were naughty or when they made mistakes with their school work.

AT ABOUT THE AGE of four, William Shakespeare would have gone to a "petty school" to learn to read. This was a small private school for boys and girls. At six, girls left the petty school to be taught at home by their mothers or, if they were rich, by private tutors. At the same age, if their parents could afford not to send them out to work, sons of middle-class men like John Shakespeare were provided with free education at the local grammar school.

The purpose of the school was to teach Latin. At the time, people needed to know Latin if they wanted to go on to university, in order to follow a career in politics, law, medicine, teaching, or the Church.

Pater noster qui es

READING MATTERS
Children learned to read using a "hornbook", a piece of wood covered with printed paper, protected by a sheet of transparent horn. This hornbook is for learning the Lord's Prayer in Latin. Every pupil had to learn this prayer by heart.

"Our Father which art in Heaven" in Latin, from the Lord's Prayer

RELUCTANT PUPILS
Most boys hated going to school. The hours were long, the lessons were dull, and their behaviour was strictly controlled. "When I should have been at school," wrote author Thomas Nashe in 1592, "I was close under a hedge or under a barn playing at Jack-in-the-box."

19th-century painting illustrating Jaques's speech about a whining schoolboy in *As You Like It*

With his hornbook and satchel, the boy described in As You Like It *sets off "unwillingly to school"*

Feathers tended to get in the way, but were sometimes left on for show

"And then the whining schoolboy, with his satchel, and shining morning face, creeping like a snail unwillingly to school."

WILLIAM SHAKESPEARE
Jaques in *As You Like It*

The pen had to be dipped into the ink at regular intervals

PEN AND INK
Before children could begin learning to write, they had to make themselves a pen called a quill from a goose feather. They trimmed the feather to the right shape and size using a "penknife", then cut the tip at an angle to make a nib. Ink was kept in a pot called an inkwell, made of sheep's horn, pottery, wood, or metal.

Horn inkwells

A selection of goose-feather quills

BALANCING ACT
There were no desks in Tudor schools, so pupils had to rest their work on their knees. This was no problem when they were reading from text books and hornbooks, but it must have made things very difficult when they had to practise their handwriting! In the petty school, children sat on stools, but grammar school boys sat on long benches called forms.

As he reads, the schoolboy follows the words with his finger

TRAGIC INSPIRATION
At school, Shakespeare was introduced to the work of ancient Roman authors such as Seneca (4 BC–65 AD). Seneca wrote serious plays called tragedies, which dealt with the suffering and death of great heroes. When Shakespeare grew up to be a writer, one of his first plays was a bloodthirsty tragedy inspired by Seneca called *Titus Andronicus*.

OLD FAVOURITE
Shakespeare's favourite writer was the poet Ovid (43 BC–17 AD), whose poem *Metamorphoses* is a collection of stories drawn from ancient Greek and Roman myths. In 1598, a writer called Francis Meres compared Shakespeare to Ovid, "The sweet witty soul of Ovid lives in mellifluous and honey-tongued Shakespeare."

Religious conflict

THE 16TH CENTURY was a time of bitter religious divisions. All English people were Christian, but there were two rival versions of the faith – Catholicism and Protestantism. In 1534, Henry VIII broke with the Catholic Church and declared himself head of an Anglican, or English, Church. Under his son Edward VI (1547–53), the Anglican Church became Protestant. There was a swing back to Catholicism under Mary (1553–58), but Elizabeth (1588–1603) restored Protestantism, fining anyone who refused to worship in an Anglican church. The Protestants were split into Anglicans and Puritans, people who thought the break with Catholics had not gone far enough.

Mary, crowned Queen of Heaven, holds the baby Jesus

AN ENGLISH BIBLE
The Bible that Shakespeare knew is known as the Geneva Bible. Catholics used a Latin Bible, but Protestants thought that everyone should be able to read the book in their own language. When Mary came to the throne, a group of Protestants fled to Geneva, where they wrote this English translation.

QUEEN OF HEAVEN
Catholics prayed in front of statues of saints, such as Mary the mother of Christ, whom they called the Queen of Heaven. Protestants said that there were no special saints in heaven, and they condemned religious statues as idols. Under the Protestant king, Edward VI, statues like this one were smashed to pieces all over England.

COUNTING PRAYERS
Rosary beads were used by Catholics to keep count of prayers. Catholics believed that the repetition of certain Latin prayers, such as Ave Maria, or Hail Mary, would help them to get to heaven. Protestants said that this was superstition.

Leather carrying case

BODY AND BLOOD
Catholics believed that their priests had the power to turn bread and wine into the body and blood of Christ. Priests carried portable communion sets like this to perform the ceremony for Catholics worshipping in secret. Anglican priests performed a similar ceremony, but they did not believe that the bread and wine were really changed into Christ's body and blood.

Chalice for giving wine at communion

Plate for communion wafers

Christ depicted on the cross

Bottle for carrying wine

BLOODY MARY
Queen Mary had almost 290 Protestants burned at the stake, and fellow Protestants celebrated them as martyrs – heroes who died for their faith. The queen was nicknamed "Bloody Mary". Elizabeth had 193 Catholics executed. They were killed not for their beliefs, but for treason, since they were loyal to a foreign ruler, the Pope.

The lamb, a sacrificial animal, stands for Christ, whom Christians believe sacrificed himself to save humanity

Simple cross

Richly decorated Catholic cross

At each end of the cross are portraits of Matthew, Mark, Luke, and John, authors of the Christian Gospels

A Puritan father gives his family religious instruction

PLOTS AGAINST THE QUEEN
In 1587, Queen Elizabeth had her cousin, Mary Stuart, Queen of Scots, executed. Mary, a Catholic, had been a prisoner in England since 1568, when she fled from Scotland after being defeated in battle by the Scottish Protestants. She was beheaded after becoming the focus of a series of plots by English Catholics. They had planned to murder Elizabeth and replace her with Mary. Such plots were encouraged by the Pope, the head of the Catholic Church, who had declared in 1570 that Elizabeth was no longer the rightful queen.

PURITAN BELIEFS
Puritans wanted to strip away all the features of Christian worship that did not appear in the Bible. They thought that the Anglican Church should get rid of bishops, vestments, or church clothes, and all elaborate ceremonies, which they called "popish practices". Many Puritans rejected the use of the crucifix, a cross depicting the crucifixion of Christ, as a Christian symbol. They disapproved of jewelled crosses.

MIXED BELIEFS
Catholics and Anglicans both used the cross on which Christ died as a symbol of their faith, although Catholic crosses were more highly decorated. It is hard to tell what Shakespeare would have thought of this cross. In the late 17th century, a writer called Richard Davies said that Shakespeare "died a Papist" (Catholic). His plays do show certain Catholic features, such as characters that swear by saints. However, one play, *King John*, is strongly anti-Catholic. We don't know what Shakespeare really believed. Perhaps, like many English people, he had a mixture of beliefs.

A country childhood

W ILLIAM S HAKESPEARE grew up in the heart of the countryside. He knew the farmers' fields around Stratford, the meadows where wild flowers grew, and the Forest of Arden to the north. As an adult writing plays in London, Shakespeare drew on his memories of the countryside. His plays are full of accurate descriptions of flowers, trees, wild birds and animals, clouds, and the changing seasons. In *Macbeth*, Shakespeare describes night falling with the words, "Light thickens, and the crow makes wing to the rooky wood," and in *Romeo and Juliet*, Capulet, hearing of his daughter's death, says, "Death lies on her like an untimely frost upon the sweetest flower in all the field."

LITTLE LIVESTOCK
Farm animals were smaller in Shakespeare's time than they are now. Some of today's rare breeds give us an idea of what they looked like. The Bagot goat has not changed since 1380, when King Richard II gave a herd to Sir John Bagot.

Longhorn

Livestock

In the 1500s, farm animals had many uses. Cattle were milked and used to pull ploughs. Sheep provided wool, meat, and milk. Goats were used for milk, meat, horn, and leather. In November, when most livestock was killed because animal feed was in short supply, pigs were fed on acorns in the woods, to provide a valuable source of fresh meat for the end of the winter.

"When icicles hang by the wall, And Dick the shepherd blows his nail, And Tom bears logs into the hall, And milk comes frozen home in pail..."

WILLIAM SHAKESPEARE
Winter in *Love's Labours Lost*

Bagot goat